Whore

Home Wrecker

Saint

Concubine

Victim

Lover

Reformist

Martyr

Witch

Feminist

Adulteress

Vixen

Temptress

?

Introduction to Hever Castle

Anne Boleyn is a lot of things to a lot of people. She's right up there as one of the most controversial female figures in history. At worst, she's seen as a whore and home wrecker. At best, she's portrayed as a saint and victim. But with two such divergent images it's difficult to say who she really was. The truth is likely somewhere in between.

A great place to explore the real life of Anne Boleyn is her childhood home Hever Castle in Kent, England. If you've managed to find your way to Hever Castle, then skip to the tour guide section of this book on page 21. Or if you have time, find a nice tree in the gardens to sit under and read up on the life of Anne Boleyn first.

Disclosure: while I am not a historian, I am a passionate student of history. Anne Boleyn was born more than five hundred years ago, which is a long time in history. Because of this, sometimes we don't know exactly what happened. All we can do is conjecture based on the facts that we do know, and leave it up to historians (and dreamers!) to fill in the gaps.

This is a book about the life of the influential women who lived at Hever Castle (most notably Anne Boleyn) and a practical tour guide for your visit. At the end of the book you'll find a bibliography and other resources to help you in your history studies. I invite you to form your own conclusions about the cast of characters that have called Hever Castle home and I hope that this is just the beginning of your historic journey.

Godspeed.

— Katherine Longhi

Getting to Hever Castle

Hever Castle is 30 miles from London in West Kent.

To get to Hever Castle, trains run from London Victoria and London Bridge (via Oxted or East Croydon) to Edenbridge Town Station. From Edenbridge rail station you can take taxi three miles to the castle.

In order to spend more time at Hever Castle, and less time waiting for a taxi you should book one in advance. You can call either:

Relyon Taxis 01732 863800

or Edenbridge Cars 01732 864009

If you are brave enough to drive, simply enter the post code TN8 7NG into your navigation system.

If you are brave enough to drive without a navigation system (or you are a Boy Scout,) take the M25 and exit at junctions 5 or 6. From either exit, the brown signs to the castle are easy enough to follow.

No matter which way you drive, be prepared that the roads are very, very narrow. If you think you're going the wrong way, you're probably going the right way.

Elizabeth I Family Tree

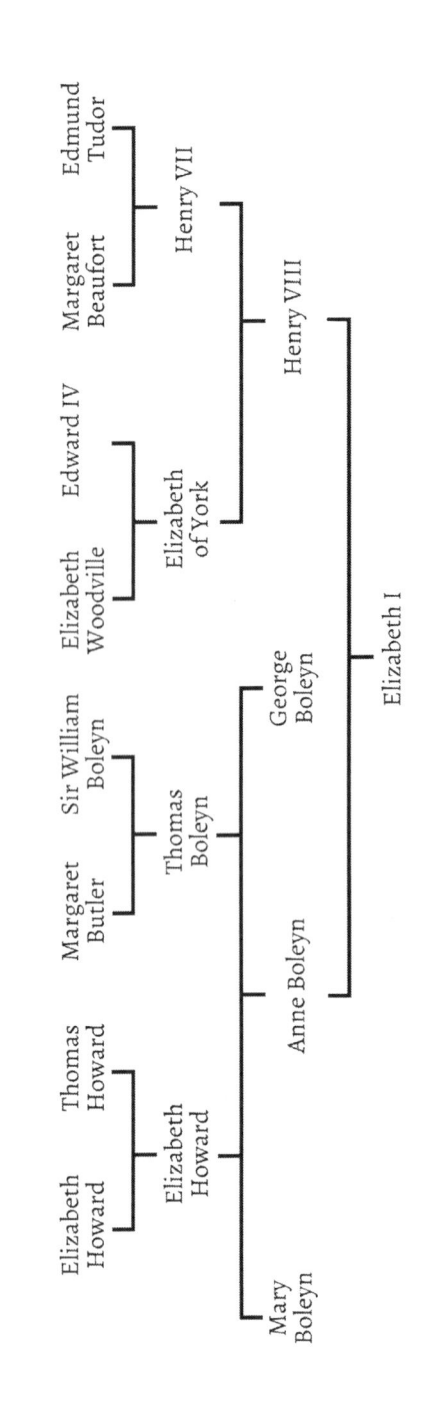

- Elizabeth Howard
- Thomas Howard
  └ Elizabeth Howard
- Margaret Butler
- Sir William Boleyn
  └ Thomas Boleyn
- Elizabeth Woodville
- Edward IV
  └ Elizabeth of York
- Margaret Beaufort
- Edmund Tudor
  └ Henry VII

- Mary Boleyn
- Anne Boleyn
- George Boleyn

(Thomas Boleyn × Elizabeth Howard → Anne Boleyn)
(Elizabeth of York × Henry VII → Henry VIII)

Anne Boleyn × Henry VIII → Elizabeth I

House of Tudor

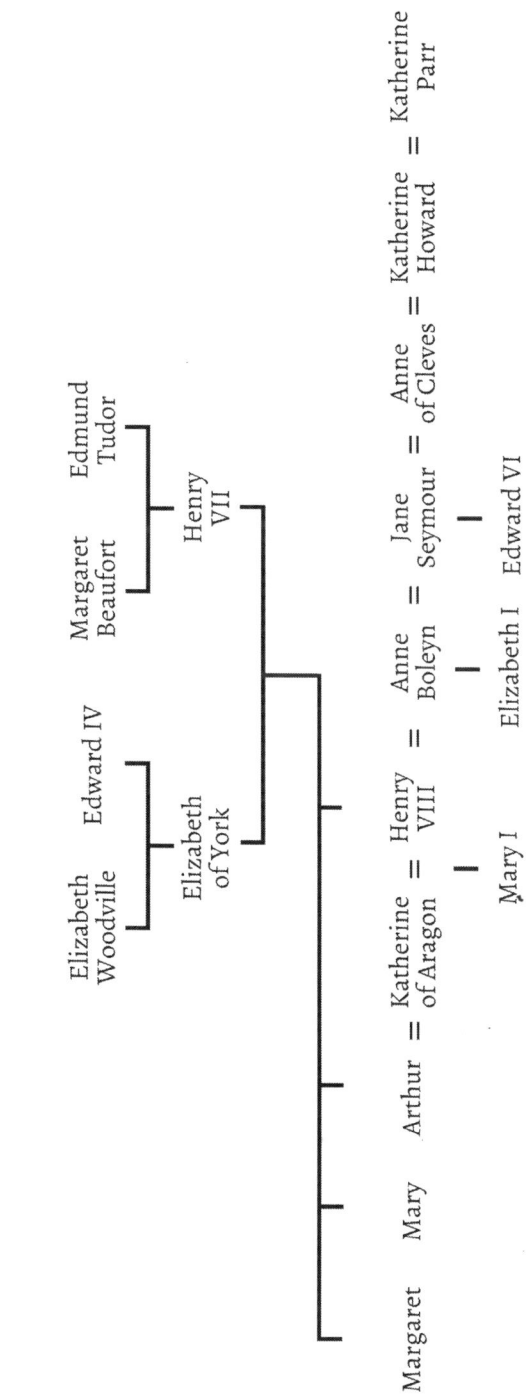

```
                    Elizabeth    Edward IV      Margaret    Edmund
                    Woodville                   Beaufort    Tudor
                         └────┬────┘                 └────┬────┘
                              │                           │
                         Elizabeth                     Henry
                          of York              =        VII
                                    ┌──────────┴──────────┐
    ┌──────────┬──────────┬─────────┴─┐
Margaret    Mary     Arthur  =  Katherine  Henry  =  Anne    Jane    = Anne     = Katherine = Katherine
                              of Aragon    VIII    Boleyn   Seymour    of Cleves   Howard     Parr
                                              │        │        │
                                           Mary I  Elizabeth I  Edward VI
```

Anne's Life

Anne Boleyn's earliest controversy started on her original birthday. This is because historians can't actually agree on the date and place. They do however agree that the year was either 1501 or 1507. At the time of Anne's birth, women weren't deemed important enough for their births to be entered into public record. Not even aristocratic women like Anne who would become the Queen of England.

Anne's father, Thomas Boleyn, inherited Hever Castle from his father, William, in 1505. Thomas is often portrayed as an evil schemer, using his children and family purely for his own advancement at court. Of course, this was the name of the game during Tudor times. You can hardly blame Thomas for doing what any other man of his time would have done in his position. There were different standards at the time.

A quick look at the highlights of Thomas' career:

- 1509 Knighted

- 1512 Sent as ambassador to the Low Countries

- 1517 Escorted Henry VIII's sister Margaret, on her visit to England from Scotland where she had been queen consort for ten years.

- 1519 Appointed as Ambassador to France

- 1521 Appointed as Ambassador to Spain

- 1523 Made Knight of the Garter

- 1525 Made Lord Rochford.

- 1529 Sent as envoy to seek support for the divorce of Henry VIII and Katherine of Aragon from Emperor Charles V and Pope Clement VII (a particularly important task considering he was helping pave the way for his daughter Anne to be Queen of England.)

- 1519 Made Earl of Ormonde and Wiltshire

- 1530 Succeeded Cardinal Wolsey as Lord Privy Seal. After the king, this was the highest position in the land. In fact, in the capacity of Lord Privy Seal, Wolsey had basically run the country for the first 10 years of the young King

Henry VIII's reign.

You have to understand the family and parents that Anne Boleyn was born into to have a deeper understanding for how she wound up in the big mess that was her life. Like her father, Anne was ambitious. Normally the adjective ambitious has a bad connotation to it, especially for a woman at that time. However, at the most basic level having ambition simply means that you want more in life than what you have already, and that you're prepared to work very hard to get there.

Thomas Boleyn married Lady Elizabeth Howard, eldest daughter of Thomas Howard, the Earl of Surrey (and later the 2nd Duke of Norfolk) around 1498 or 1499. Through her father, Elizabeth was a direct descendant of King Edward I. When Elizabeth was a young girl she entered the service of Henry VIII's mother, Queen Elizabeth of York. When Henry succeeded his father as king, Elizabeth went on to serve Queen Katherine of Aragon.

Some people say that Elizabeth was a bit of a cougar and had an affair with young King Henry when he first came to the throne. However, Henry always denied it. Henry may have bedded both of her daughters, but Henry drew the line at Elizabeth Howard.

All of Thomas and Elizabeth's children who survived childhood were terribly scandalous. As the oldest of the siblings, Mary was the first Boleyn child to cause scandal. She served Mary Tudor in France from 1514 and had an affair with King Francis. He used to call her "my English mare."

Mary's parents brought her back to England in 1520 and married her off to William Carey in an effort to reduce the scandal. Unfortunately, the plan backfired because returning to the English court put Mary in close proximity to the English king. She subsequently had an affair with him too.

After Mary's husband died in 1528, no other man would go near her. She was damaged goods after her affair with Henry VIII. Mary decided to elope with a poor commoner, William Stafford, in 1535. Lucky for her she was banished from court just in time to escape all of the beheadings. Mary was the only Boleyn child of Thomas and Elizabeth to keep her head.

Younger brother, George Boleyn, was not so lucky in his fate but his start in life seemed promising. Whereas Anne and Mary were educated at home, George was sent to Oxford for his education. He started his career at court hoping to be a successful courtier like his father. By 1525 George was unhappily married to Lady Jane Parker and promoted to the King's Privy Council.

George's career wasn't too bad. It didn't hurt that his sister Anne had caught the eye of the king. Some of his titles and roles include:

- Royal Cupbearer
- Master of the King's Buckhounds
- Chief Steward of Beaulieu, Essex
- Diplomat sent on missions to France in order to help Henry get his divorce from Katherine of Aragon and later to negotiate a marriage contract between the Princess Elizabeth and the third son of the king of France
- Viscount Rochford
- Constable of Dover Castle
- Warden of the Cinque Ports

Now on to Anne. What was it like for her growing up? A typical Tudor girl's education would have normally involved sewing, spinning, and the usual female crafts as well as religious studies. The very fortunate ladies would have been sent away to the courts of Europe to learn languages and the ways of court life. Anne was one of these lucky ladies to essentially receive a princess's education. Anne's classrooms of study were the courts of Margaret of Austria and Queen Claude of France. Her education was on par with that of Katherine of Aragon, her predecessor as Queen of England.

Anne's first experience at a European court was the Palace of Mechelen, in present day Belgium where Margaret of Austria was Governor of the Habsburg Netherlands. Margaret was a powerful woman and her court was known for its culture, its courtly love tradition, education, vast library and Margaret's collections of paintings, illuminated manuscripts and music books. Anne was only there for a year but it probably made a big impression on a young girl to be in such a place. Equally, Anne made a big impression on Queen Margaret and she wrote to Anne's father as such.

"I find in her so fine a spirit, and so perfect an address for a lady of her years, that I am more beholden to you for sending her than you can be to me for receiving her." (Weir 2007)

Next stop on Anne's European court tour was the French Court of Queen Claude. This was actually an upgrade for Anne as she behaved so well at Margaret's court that she got recommended for a position in the more prestigious French court.

Queen Claude of France was famous for her piety and she was very strict that her ladies-in-waiting conform to her standard. Her court was essentially a noble school for ladies. Whilst Claude was busy teaching her ladies how to be wise and virtuous, her husband King Francis I was busy trying to deflower them. According to the sixteenth-century French historian Seigneur de Brantome "Rarely, or ever, did any maid or wife leave that court chaste." As the king's lover, Mary Boleyn proved the rule. Anne's behaviour is less widely known, so either she was the exception to the rule or she was more discreet.

Anne's behaviour at the French court was only called into question in the last few weeks of Anne's life when the charges of her offences against the king were laid at her door. It was only then that King Francis actually told Anne's uncle, the Duke of Norfolk, that Anne hadn't exactly been chaste during her time at the French court. Around the same time Henry VIII told the Spanish ambassador that he knew Anne had been corrupted in France. Apparently Anne's knowledge of sex was more than what Henry expected from a virgin. Conveniently, he hadn't complained at the time!

After Anne's rather muddled education at the French court, she returned to England in 1521 because a marriage between her and James Butler had been arranged to settle a dispute of land and the title of Earl of Ormonde. The marriage never took place. Perhaps by that time Henry wanted Anne for himself and blocked the marriage, or at least he wanted her to stay single a little while longer.

Anne's first recorded public appearance at the English court was in 1522. She played the part of Perseverance at the pageant of "The Château Vert" at York Place. Pageants were a big deal in those days. They were the Tudor equivalent to a Broadway musical minus the plot. Pageants were a great way for noble ladies to stand out in the court and show off their musical, dancing, and theatrical skills. Plus it helped them meet eligible men on the marriage market.

Promptly after Anne's debut at court, she fell in love and agreed to marry Henry Percy, heir to the earldom of Northumberland. The flames of the pair's love were promptly extinguished by their families and Cardinal Wolsey. Percy was considered above Anne's station but worse he was already betrothed to Mary Talbot. The marriage between Percy and Mary Talbot already had the royal seal of approval and therefore had to go ahead, despite the fact that the pair hated each other. Anne on the other hand retreated to Hever Castle to recover from the scandal and nurse her broken heart.

Sidenote: Anne never forgave Cardinal Wolsey for his part in preventing her marriage to Henry Percy and humiliating her on account of her station in life. Years later when Anne was secure on her path to becoming queen, she watched with glee as Henry seized all of Wolsey's property and arrested him. Wolsey died on his way to the Tower of London in complete poverty.

So how did these two lovebirds, Henry and Anne, wind up together? Let's examine their mutual attractions.

Why Henry fancied Anne:

- She was passionate, witty, ambitious, and could go head to head with Henry in a debate.

- She was well educated and had the experience of mixing with the crème de la crème of Europe.

- She liked to go hunting with Henry and they shared other hobbies and interests.

- Although not the typical beauty by Tudor standards, Anne had famously beautiful dark eyes and comported herself with confidence and allure.

- She was all of the things a king would want in a lover: vivacious, passionate, and hot-tempered.

- She didn't care what people thought of her and was a free spirit.

Why Anne fancied Henry:

- He was tall and handsome, just 32 years old.

- He was athletic and extremely well educated.

- He was considered the prince of all princes in Europe.

- He was a real smoothie with the ladies. Case in point - here are some of his own words written to Anne in the first love letter he wrote her:

In turning over in my mind the contents of your last letters, I have put myself into great agony, not knowing how to interpret them, whether to my disadvantage, as you show in some places, or to my advantage, as I understand them in some others, beseeching you earnestly to let me know expressly your whole mind as to the love between us two.

It is absolutely necessary for me to obtain this answer, having been for above a whole year stricken with the dart of love, and not yet sure whether I shall fail of finding a place in your heart and affection, which last point has prevented me for some time past from calling you my mistress; because, if you only love me with an ordinary love, that name is not suitable for you, because it denotes a singular love, which is far from common. But if you please to do the office of a true loyal mistress and friend, and to give up yourself body and heart to me, who will be, and have been, your most loyal servant, (if your rigour does not forbid me) I promise you that not only the name shall be given you, but also that I will take you for my only mistress, casting off all others besides you out of my thoughts and affections, and serve you only. I beseech you to give an entire answer to this my rude letter, that I may know on what and how far I may depend. And if it does not please you to answer me in writing, appoint some place where I may have it by word of mouth, and I will go thither with all my heart. No more, for fear of tiring you. Written by the hand of him who would willingly remain yours, H. R.

Henry certainly gave Casanova a run for his money in the romance department. Between 1527 and 1528, Henry wrote Anne a total of 17 love letters. Henry actually despised writing so it shows how deeply in love with Anne he was.

It may seem pretty obvious in hindsight, but the qualities that Henry and Anne admired in each other would change over time. There is a reason why there is a perception that Henry was a fat old tyrant of a king, and that's because that's what he became after Anne's death. The time that he spent with Anne probably had something to do with that. Also the qualities that Henry first found appealing in Anne as a lover were not exactly the same qualities he was looking for in a queen. He was just too in love with her to think about the impact that marrying Anne would have on the realm.

By 1524 it was clear that Henry's first wife, Katherine of Aragon, could no longer bear children. Also by this time Henry had a long-standing affair with his mistress Bessie Blount, and an illegitimate son by her named Henry Fitzroy. Henry never thought about putting Katherine aside for Bessie, even though she had provided him with a son. It was only when Anne came along that he strongly considered the idea of getting rid of Katherine.

The first records of Anne and Henry VIII's relationship date to 1526. At first Anne refused Henry's advances. Anne had learned the hard way from observing her sister Mary that being the king's mistress was not the way to go. Not to mention the fact that it wasn't going to be easy for Henry to get out of his marriage to Katherine of Aragon. After Anne's time at the French court, and the mishap with Henry Percy, Anne was cautious about giving her heart and body to the king. Henry on the other hand could fall in love with a different woman every day, which he practically did.

But what could Henry really do about Katherine of Aragon? As one of the most powerful kings in Europe, Henry had to be sensible about how his treatment of Katherine would impact world politics. Katherine's nephew was the Holy Roman Emperor, Charles V, and a major player on the European continent. France was the other power. Traditionally England hated France. The Hundred Years War wasn't too distant in the past. Henry didn't want to upset his great ally the Holy Roman Emperor, which was partly why he married Katherine in the first place.

In the summer of 1527, Anne left the English court and returned to Hever Castle. Henry was dismayed by Anne's departure and suspected that Anne was intentionally avoiding him. There's a reason why the expression "absence makes the heart grow fonder" exists. Perhaps Anne was trying it out. By this time, it was only a year into Henry and Anne's courtship, but Anne had already accepted to become Henry's wife.

The following summer, Anne contracted the deadly sweating sickness. Luckily for Anne, she fully recovered. During this time Henry was beside himself with worry. Although he wasn't quite worried enough to actually visit Anne at Hever Castle. Henry's fear of catching the disease seemed to be stronger than his love for Anne.

With Anne's recovery and her relationship with Henry continuing to heat up, Henry's attempts to get out of his marriage to Katherine of Aragon became increasingly more desperate. The subject became known as "The King's Great Matter."

Henry's first approach to ditching Katherine was to turn the subject of the validity of his marriage to into a great theological debate. Henry turned to the Bible for ammunition.

According to Leviticus 20:21, "If a man marries his brother's wife, it is an act of impurity. He has violated his brother, and the guilty couple will remain childless."

Henry tried to rely on this biblical passage as proof that his marriage to Katherine was "an act of impurity." It was true that Katherine had married Henry's older brother Arthur. However before Henry married Katherine they had gotten special dispensation from the Pope just to avoid this issue of validity in the future. It was also true that Katherine and Henry's marriage had produced more stillborn children than surviving children. Their only surviving child was the future Queen Mary I. However

Henry argued that Mary didn't count as she was not a male heir to the throne.

Katherine defended her marriage to Henry by claiming that her marriage to Arthur was not valid. During Tudor times marriage was a two step process and both had to be in place for the marriage to be valid. Step 1 was the religious service and step 2 was the consummation. The two steps were important in a time when children were often married for political reasons. They might be legally married for years before they went through with second step of marriage.

Katherine relied on the fact that her marriage to Arthur was never consummated to prove the validity of her marriage to Henry. It was her word against a dead guy's. Katherine may have had the better legal and religious arguments as to why her marriage to Henry was valid, but Henry was determined to move on from Katherine and marry Anne. Henry grossly underestimated what it would take to resolve his "Great Matter." He was a man who was used to getting what he wanted, when he wanted it. Furthermore Henry grossly underestimated Katherine's determination to save her marriage.

The official court set up to hear the trial of Henry and Katherine's marriage was called the Legatine Court and it started on 31st May 1529. During the time that the Legatine Court is in session, Anne spent her time back and forth between court and Hever Castle. On the one hand, Anne tried to stay out of the drama and preserve her reputation for when she would become queen. But on the other hand, Anne had to dash off to meet Henry whenever he would call for her.

It was around now that Katherine and Anne's views of each other started to shift. At first Katherine dismissed Anne as just another of Henry's mistresses. He'd had scores of mistresses before and Katherine's conviction that it was her destiny to remain Queen of England was strong. On the other hand, Anne initially felt pity towards her former mistress. Anne's pity changed dramatically to hatred when Anne realised that Katherine wasn't going to go away quietly.

While Anne was putting on her double act, so was Henry. During the Legatine Court Henry tried to appear to be the doting husband to Katherine. He declared that he was genuinely troubled by his marriage and if the court declared it valid that he'd be happy to return to Katherine. It seemed like Henry wasn't above lying to get his way.

While the Legatine Court was in session, the Pope intervened with his decision on the marriage. The Pope declared that Katherine was Henry's lawful wife. Henry went ballistic. At this point, Henry and Anne had been planning on getting married for three years. After this point, it would be another four years before they would finally walk down the aisle. That's a total of seven long years of courtship.

Seven years was an absolute eternity for:

- A man who was used to getting his own way to wait to marry the woman he loved

- A woman of childbearing age like Anne who knew that her and her family's happiness (and later their survival) depended on her bearing a son

- A time when the average life expectancy was half of what it is today

While the Legatine Court was in session, Team Boleyn comprising Anne, her father Thomas, now Viscount Rochford, her uncle Norfolk, and the Duke of Suffolk, were feeling edgy about Anne's delayed marriage. Suspecting that Cardinal Wolsey was involved, they plotted to take him down and put the wheels in motion. Meanwhile Henry granted Anne an upgrade to her lodgings so that she would be an easy distance whenever Henry wanted to call on her. Anne was now treated in every respect like the queen Katherine used to be and making her transition into role of queen.

To further her cause, Anne procured a copy of William Tyndale's book "The Obedience of the Christian Man and How Christian Rulers Ought to Govern." It was quite a controversial book for its time. Anne shared it with Henry and pointed out the specific passages related to the idea that a ruler is accountable to God alone and that the Church should not control a monarch. The premise of the book planted the seeds in Henry's mind that he should be absolute ruler in England, not just in government but also in religion. In the short term, the book helped Anne to get her way. However, in the longer term it created a monster out of Henry who was capable of taking her life.

But at the time, Henry and Anne were more in love than ever and essentially living like king and queen. In October 1529, Pope Clement VII wrote to Henry confirming that his marriage to Katherine was valid. The Pope pointed Henry's attention to the danger that the Turks posed to Christendom in an attempt to bury the hatchet with the errant monarch. Christians had to stick together after all, especially when there were other infidel religions threatening them. The letter further enraged Henry, and the Legatine Court ended with no result.

By November, Katherine was so disturbed by her ill treatment that she confronted Henry and complained about her "suffering the pains of Purgatory on earth." Henry showed no sympathy. He replied bluntly with three points:

- He was not her legitimate husband (therefore her treatment was nothing to do with him).

- He had many witnesses who would testify to this fact.

- If the Pope did not declare their marriage null and void, then Henry would denounce him as a heretic and marry whom he pleased.

In December Henry threw a grand party (fête) for Anne and invited several ladies of the court. Henry was still pushing the court to accept Anne as queen. Anne took her place amongst the ladies and sat next to the king, just like Katherine used to do. However, Henry celebrated Christmas with Katherine at Greenwich. Katherine's greatest allies were the people of England themselves. They loved her and Henry had to be seen at her side at Christmas to keep up appearances in front of the people.

The following year Henry avoided Katherine as much as he could. If he inadvertently bumped into her, then he would take the opportunity to try to persuade her to become a nun. Bishop Cranmer (Team Boleyn) thought that the people would accept Anne as queen by this time and told Henry to just go ahead and marry Anne. Henry started to think that he'd be justified to take Cranmer's advice. In October 1530, the Pope ordered Henry to take back Katherine but Henry ignored the order.

In January 1531, Pope Clement VII forbade Henry to remarry and threatened him with excommunication. This was a huge blow for Henry who was devoutly Catholic. In February, a convocation was ordered to recognise Henry as "sole protector and supreme head of the English church and clergy." Team Katherine comprising Nicholas Carewe, the Duke of Suffolk, the Duchess of Norfolk, Bishop Fisher, Reginald Pole, and Elizabeth Barton "the Nun of Kent," retaliated when Henry announced his plan to marry Anne.

By 1532 Anne was queen in all but name. During the New Year celebrations, Anne gave Henry a set of boar spears and he gave her a set of wall hangings. Henry forbade courtiers to give gifts to Katherine. Katherine sent Henry a gold cup which Anne promptly made him return.

In July Henry declared that the Pope had no power over him and he would marry Anne. But first Henry needed to put the finishing touches on making Anne seem as legitimate as possible. Henry bestowed on Anne the title Marquis of Pembroke. It was a big honour for Anne to be raised to a Marquis. Normally the title was reserved only for men.

For the ceremony marking her new title of Marquis, Anne dressed in jewels and ermine trimmed velvet for the lavish ceremony at Windsor Castle. You can picture her with long loose flowing hair and her beautiful clothing and jewels. The ennoblement ceremony was in a way a dress rehearsal for her coronation. Anne played her role well, in the exact way that Henry expected of his future queen.

In September work started on refurbishing the royal lodgings in the Tower of London in preparation for Anne's coronation. In order that Anne could look her best on the big day, Henry asked Katherine to return her royal jewels. She did so reluctantly knowing that Henry intended on giving them to Anne.

The next task was for Henry to get buy-in from his European peers for his potential marriage to Anne. He planned a big trip to France so that he could parade Anne around with King Francis I. Henry and Anne set sail for Calais in October. With Francis' blessing Henry asked him to meet with the Pope and push the case for the annulment of Henry's marriage to Katherine of Aragon. Francis assured Henry of his support and this gave Henry and Anne such a boost that they started living together officially when they got back to England.

Sometime during their trip to France, Anne and Henry married in secret and consummated their marriage. The exact order of events is a little hazy. Henry and Anne were no longer holding back. In February 1533 Anne publicised her pregnancy announcing that she was craving apples.

In March Anne formed her royal household. This is kind of like a bride picking bridesmaids but on a much larger scale. Anne appointed 14 ladies-in-waiting who acted as her sort of personal assistants. They kept her happy, entertained her, and ran her errands. Among them were Jane Parker, Anne's sister-in-law, and Jane Seymour, Anne's future replacement as Henry's wife and queen. Jane Seymour had also served Queen Katherine so was pretty well versed in what the job entailed.

In May Thomas Cranmer, the newly appointed Archbishop of Canterbury, pronounced that Henry's marriage to Anne was valid. Henry and Anne had married in secret so the proclamation was intended to further legitimise their marriage amongst the people. Katherine was then informed that her new title was the Dowager Princess of Wales. Now there was little remaining evidence that Katherine of Aragon was ever Queen of England. However, she referred to herself as the Queen of England until her death three years later.

On 1st June 1533 Anne was crowned queen at Westminster Abbey. Finally she had everything that she ever wanted: a loving husband, the title of queen, and a baby on the way.

On 7th September 1533 Princess Elizabeth, the future Elizabeth I, was born. Anne couldn't be happier. She took the baby Elizabeth everywhere she went and doted on her like no other mother. Anne even tried to breastfeed the baby, at which point Henry stepped in to stop her. Breastfeeding was seen as being beneath a queen at that time. Henry couldn't help being disappointed at the birth of a daughter. But he and Anne were young, and a son would undoubtedly follow.

In 1534 the Act of Supremacy was passed making Henry the Supreme Head of the Church of England. Next followed the Act of Succession which made the offspring of Henry and Anne the only lawful heirs to the throne. This was another blow to Katherine and Princess Mary. The same summer Anne miscarried a baby and Henry started to have problems with impotency. The cracks were starting to show in Henry and Anne's marriage. The following year Anne became pregnant again. Henry finally had everything that he wanted except his precious male heir. And his marriage to Anne had collateral damage.

1536 was the year of years. It all unraveled very quickly for everyone involved.

- 7th January - Katherine of Aragon died at Kimbolton Castle. Anne temporarily rejoiced thinking that her problems were finally over. Accusations that Anne had poisoned her former mistress spread like wildfire. Today it is accepted that it was probably cancer that killed Katherine at the ripe age of fifty. To mark the occasion of Katherine's death, Henry and Anne dressed in yellow (the official colour of mourning in Spain) and celebrated.

- 24th January - Henry fell off his horse and was knocked unconscious for around 2 hours. Anne and the entire court panicked.

- 29th January - Anne caught Jane Seymour sitting on Henry's knee and she miscarried her saviour - a boy around 15 weeks old. This left Anne dangerously exposed and distraught.

- March - Anne picked a fight with Cromwell over the dissolution of the monasteries. They are united in their mutual hatred for each other. Anne hated seeing money from religious houses going into Cromwell's pocket. Cromwell hated Anne's interference. He started to plot to bring her down and enlisted help by bringing over courtiers from Team Katherine to Team Jane.

- 24th April - with the King's approval, a formal investigation was launched to investigate treason and other offences committed by Anne and others.

- 30th April - Mark Smeaton, a lowly musician in Anne's household, was arrested for committing adultery with the queen. Smeaton confessed after 24 hours of interrogation and torture.

- 2nd May - three more men were arrested and charged. Anne's own brother George was arrested for incest and treason. Henry began to have secret meetings with Jane Seymour to discuss the details of their marriage.

- 12th May - the four men appeared in court. They all pleaded "not guilty" except for Smeaton who pleaded "guilty" to adultery, but "not guilty" to the other charges. It didn't matter what they pleaded, they were all found guilty and sentenced to "drawing, hanging and quartering" the ugliest and most painful way to go.

- 13th May - Anne's royal household was broken up before her trial. Around the same time, Henry told Jane that Anne will be found guilty.

- 15th May - Anne and George were tried. Both pleaded "not guilty" but were found guilty anyways. The whole thing was a set up. As a queen, Anne got the privilege of being tried by a jury of her peers who all hated her. The trial was a pure formality. Anne received a death sentence.

- 17th May - the four men were beheaded on Tower Green along with George Boleyn. George had the good fortune to be beheaded first, as he was the most senior in rank. The rest of the men followed one by one until at last poor Smeaton was practically slipping on everyone else's blood.

- 18th May 9am - Anne prepared herself to go to the scaffold on time. However, the Constable of the Tower of London, William Kingston, informed Anne that her execution was postponed for three hours due to the late arrival of the executioner.

- 18th May afternoon - Archbishop Cranmer convened an ecclesiastic court who confirmed that Henry and Anne's marriage was null and void. They also granted Henry a dispensation to marry Jane Seymour. Princess Elizabeth joined her half-sister Mary in the illegitimate club. Anne's execution was delayed again until the following morning.

Finally the next morning rolled around. Anne was informed that her marriage to Henry had been declared null and void and her daughter Elizabeth was now illegitimate. Anne probably concentrated all of her efforts on her daughter and that she had the best possible chance in life considering the stigma that Anne's death would permanently attach to Elizabeth. When it came to Anne's scaffold speech, Anne stuck to the standard script:

Good Christian people, I am come hither to die, for according to the law, and by the law I am judged to die, and therefore I will speak nothing against it. I am come hither to accuse no man, nor to speak anything of that, whereof I am accused and condemned to die, but I pray God save the king and send him long to reign over you, for a gentler nor a more merciful prince was there never: and to me he was ever a good, a gentle and sovereign lord. And if any person will meddle of my cause, I require them to judge the best. And thus I take my leave of the world and of you all, and I heartily desire you all to pray for me. O Lord have mercy on me, to God I commend my soul.

Anne then paid her executioner £20 and pardoned him for the dastardly deed he was about to commit against her. Anne knelt, said a prayer, and then her life was over before she would have even realised. The executioner distracted Anne at the last moment so that she looked away from him and probably never saw the sword coming at her. The very moment of Anne's death was probably the most humane part of the whole thing. Anne's body was wrapped and taken to the Church of St Peter ad Vincula where she was buried in an unmarked grave. Such a tragic end for such a remarkable lady who was so vivacious in life.

The next day on 20th May 1536 Henry announced his betrothal to Jane Seymour. Ten days later Henry and Jane married at Hampton Court. Whereas Anne and Henry had to wait 7 long years before they could marry, Jane and Henry only had to wait a little over 7 months. Times were changing very rapidly in Tudor England.

What really defines Anne's character is not that bad things happened to her, but how she conducted herself in the face of adversity. For example when she learned of her death sentence her response was composed and thoughtful:

I do not say that I have always borne towards the King the humility which I owed him, considering his kindness and the great honour he showed me and the great respect he always paid me; I admit too, that often I have taken it into my head to be jealous of him… But may God be my witness if I have done him any other wrong.

The day before her execution Anne sent a message to Henry:

Commend me to his Majesty, and tell him that he has ever been constant in his career of advancing me. From a private gentlewoman he made me a marchioness, from a marchioness a Queen; and now that he has no higher degree of honour left, he gives my innocence the crown of martyrdom as a saint in heaven.

Anne was gracious and grateful up until the very end of her life. But the perplexing issue is how could Henry, who was so in love with Anne, who chased her for seven long years, who wrote her love letter after love letter, who started a whole new religion for her, treat Anne so cruelly and take her life? I guess the only person who really knows that is Henry himself. At some point he decided to favour other people over Anne such as:

- Thomas Cromwell - Henry's chief minister and strong advocate for the English Reformation. Originally Anne and Thomas had common religious views but they disagreed on the details.

- Eustace Chapuys - Imperial Ambassador of the Holy Roman Emperor to England. More of a gossip than anything else, he was very vocal and critical of everything Anne did. He made sure to report all of her comings and goings to Charles V and kindly referred to her in all of his correspondence as "The Concubine."

- Catholics - Although Anne was very devout she alienated a lot of powerful men of the cloth.

- The Seymour family - there is no evidence to suggest that they were actively involved in Anne's demise but by pushing Jane towards Henry they acted indirectly on Anne.

Ultimately the king himself is the most culpable in Anne's downfall. He lets himself be persuaded by the rubbish evidence he was being fed by his inner circle. He's also less patient than he was with Katherine about producing a son. After Anne miscarries a few times Henry acts quickly when he gets the chance to remove her.

After Anne's death, sad times fell on Hever Castle. Anne's disgraced father died 2 years later and the property passed to the Crown. Henry gave Hever Castle to his 4th wife, Anne of Cleves, who by this time was going under the moniker of "The King's Beloved Sister."

Anne Boleyn's greatest contribution to this world was her daughter Elizabeth I, who ushered in the Golden Age in England and ruled for over 40 years, alone, with no man. Not bad for a woman. Clearly Elizabeth had some of her mother's personality traits like courage and determination.

Are you ready to explore Hever Castle and see where the real Anne Boleyn lived? Great! Read on.

Hever Castle Rooms

Hever Castle came into the Boleyn family when Anne's great grandfather Geoffrey bought the castle in 1462. At the time, it was already a couple hundred years old. So you are about to visit a castle that is in the region of 700 years old. You sometimes see Anne's family referred to as the Bullen family. This is because that's how they spelled their name during their time. Bullen evolved over the centuries into Boleyn.

With the decline of the Boleyn family after Anne's death in 1536, Hever Castle itself also went into decline. First with the Waldegrave family who owned Hever Castle from 1557 and then under the Meade Waldo family from 1749 until 1903. I don't think anyone can even begin to fathom the work and cost that goes into maintaining a giant old castle.

Finally a gentleman from New York, William Waldorf Astor, swooped in and purchased Hever Castle in 1903. When he bought it, it wasn't much to look at it. But slowly over a few decades, with modernisation and care, Astor managed to restore the castle to its former Tudor splendour.

Astor was the man with the money but the man with the vision was the architect who restored the castle, F.L. Pearson. Together they were the dream team.

There are two distinct styles of rooms in the castle - those in Tudor style which were recreated by Astor and those in the style of Astor's day - Edwardian (think like what you would have seen on the Titanic). However, even the Edwardian style rooms have a little Tudor inspiration in them.

When you enter through the portcullis, which is the entrance way with a large spiky door, head through the courtyard. Pass through the door and turn right into the Inner Hall.

Inner Hall

When you enter the Inner Hall you're going to have to use your imagination a bit. Although you see a grand hall in the Tudor style today, during Anne's time this was actually a kitchen. Close your eyes for a moment. Inhale the smell of steak and ale pie cooking over a fire. Now listen to the clanking and hustle and bustle as the kitchen staff scurry around to make a meal fit for King Henry VIII. Indeed Henry did make a few impromptu appearances at Hever Castle when he called upon Anne and her family.

Now open your eyes and look up at the balcony. The Italian walnut paneling was designed by the sculptor William Silver Frith in 1905. Fantastic isn't it?

Directly overhead you'll see a wonderful plaster ceiling designed by Nathaniel Hitch in the early 20th Century which incorporates the Tudor Rose. Keep your eyes open during your visit. You'll see the Tudor Rose incorporated into many aspects of Hever Castle.

Next check out the fireplace. To the left is a portrait of the Lady Anne Boleyn herself. To the right is a portrait of her older sister, Mary Boleyn. Mary was famous, or rather infamous for being the mistress of two kings: King Francis I of France, as well as Anne's future husband, King Henry VIII.

On the mantel piece is a clock which is a replica of the present Henry gave to Anne to celebrate their marriage. It's such a lovely and ornate gift. Instead of reading the time on it you can read into it the tragedy and irony that the couple would not be passing the rest of their lives together. There's no Romeo and Juliet here. Dry your eyes.

Drawing Room

Surprised? Not exactly Tudor is it?

This room was created for William Waldorf Astor (aka the saviour of Hever Castle) at the turn of the last century. Astor was rich and famous (of the New York Astor family) and he had a penchant for England and castles. Astor had become disillusioned with New York. According to him it "was no longer a fit place for a gentleman to live."

As the owner of Hever Castle, Astor took his mission to restore the castle to its previous Tudor splendour very seriously. He visited many Tudor buildings for inspiration. Also he was insistent that the workers (no fewer than 800 plasterers, carpenters, stoneworkers, metal workers, etc) should do their work with the same tools and in the same way that actual Tudor craftsmen would have done. Rulers and levellers were banned. You won't see any perfectly straight edges here. Everything was done by eye!

Take a look at the spectacular paneling of oak inlaid with bog oak and holly on the walls. This feature was inspired by a trip Astor took to Sizergh Castle in Cumbria. Look at the ceiling. Can you find a straight edge?

The Astor family was the toast of the town (even if they were Yankees) and this room is where they entertained guests and plied them with drinks before dinner. The drinks were hidden behind the wall at the far end of the room. Either William didn't trust his guests could hold their liquor, or he felt that it was more sophisticated to be out of sight. Maybe a bit of both.

The Great Hall

This room was used as a dining room when Anne and her family lived here. When Henry VIII called on Anne (usually with little notice) it was not a small task for Anne's mother Lady Boleyn to prepare the castle for the royal entourage. Her 50-strong staff were not nearly enough people for the job. All of the bedrooms had to be prepared (and their normal occupants sent elsewhere) and the ingredients to prepare lavish meals had to be procured.

Look also at the fireplace. The tapestry has Henry's coat of arms on it and was brought from Hampton Court. The Boleyn coat of arms is carved in the stone above the fireplace. Take a good look and now compare it to this one of Anne's:

Do you see the difference?

Anne had more royal connections on her mother's side of the family so her coat of arms reflects that. Henry designed Anne's coat of arms so she really didn't have any say, although she did choose her own motto "Most Happy." At least she was up until the very end.

Imagine being a guest here at a meal presided over by King Henry VIII. You've got a royal duchess to your right and a member of the Privy Council to your left. King

Henry is sitting at the far end of the room on a raised platform so that he has the best view of the room. Music is streaming down from the balcony above. If you look up, you can see the minstrels playing their instruments.

As you leave the room, check out the giant gilt door locks. One of them is real, and one of them is fake (don't touch either of them). The real one belonged to Henry VIII himself. Henry didn't trust anyone else's locks but his own. Looks like he forgot to take his lock with him the last time he left Hever Castle. You know you're a rich king when you can go around leaving your locks everywhere.

After you pass through the door to leave, look at the marker to your left with the year 1968 carved on it. In that year there was a massive flood that came all the way up to this marker in the castle. Another huge project for the Astor family!

The Library

The library would have been an estate office during the Boleyn times so there's not too much to note about this room from that time period.

However, there's a very important man in the portrait hanging over the fireplace. Without this man's money Hever Castle wouldn't be what it is today. And he never even set foot in Hever Castle. I'm not talking about William Waldorf Astor, but rather the founder of the Astor dynasty - Johann Jakob Astor, who was later known as John Jacob Astor.

The library is a fitting place for William's great grandfather's portrait to hang. John was born the poor son of a butcher in 1763 in Walldorf, Germany. He emigrated to the US after the end of the American Revolutionary War and made a killing (proverbially speaking) in trade and eventually real estate when he bought up loads of land on a little island called Manhattan. He was the right man, in the right place, at the right time. So here is John's portrait in a lush library amongst thousands of books. This room is where distinguished gentlemen like Sir Arthur Conan Doyle, author of Sherlock Holmes, would have retired after a nice dinner in the Great Hall.

Before you leave, take a good look at the ceiling. It's another inspiration from Hampton Court Palace.

Morning Room

You are now entering the ladies' zone of the Tudor times. This was a private retiring room where Anne, her mother and sister probably spent a lot of time doing female things like sewing, spinning, and gossiping.

Anne and Mary were just like any other set of sisters. They played together and bickered together. They had a huge falling out in 1534 when Queen Anne banished Mary from court after she married William Stafford without permission from either Anne or Henry. William was much lower in rank than Mary and deemed unacceptable to marry into the queen's family. Anne, her brother and her father devoted themselves to improving the family's fortune and Mary didn't seem to want to play ball. Mary was the black sheep of the family.

Take a look at the initials "HW" carved into the fireplace. They stand for Henry Waldegrave who took over Hever Castle after Anne of Cleves died in 1557. Anne of Cleves was given Hever Castle after Henry divorced her. She didn't spend a lot of time at Hever Castle, probably because it reminded her of Anne Boleyn and how easily she could have met the same fate. The wood panelling in the room is Elizabethan and was therefore likely installed by the Waldegrave family.

Before you leave to walk up the spiral staircase check out the closet in the corner. This is where the Waldegraves hid their priest. After the reign of Queen Mary it wasn't acceptable to be Catholic anymore, so the Waldegraves had to hide their true religion and made sure no one found out about the Catholic priest they worshiped with. Allegedly a priest met his maker while hiding in the little room.

©Hever Castle

Anne Boleyn's Bedroom

Like the Morning Room, this is another room where Anne would have spent a lot of time. She would have spent a lot of time here sleeping. Probably with Mary.

Through the window you can see the Tudor Village or Astor Wing of the castle. When Anne lived here she would have seen a large expanse of countryside.

Take a close look at Anne's bedhead. It's called a "made up" piece because it is literally made up of old cupboards and chests. It was bought by William Waldorf Astor when he was trying to find appropriate Tudor furniture for the room. Whoever sold it to him was trying to pull a fast one. Although "Part of Anne Boleyn's Bed from Hever 1520" is inscribed on it, the bedhead actually dates from the 17th century. Therefore it is impossible that it was Anne's.

A big clue that the bedhead didn't belong to Anne is in the coat of arms. The lion and the unicorn make up the coat of arms of James I of England and Ireland. James was Anne's daughter Elizabeth I's cousin twice removed and her successor to the throne. It would seem unlikely that Anne would have the coat of arms of a king who wasn't even born during her lifetime in her childhood bedroom.

Examine the small portrait of Anne on the wall. This is an actual original portrait painted in 1534 when Anne was Queen of England. Very few original portraits have survived. This is a truly remarkable painting.

Before you leave the room look at the portrait of Anne above the fireplace. It dates from the 1790's and is a reproduction of a Hans Holbein sketch by the Italian artist Francesco Barolozzi. With her long flowing hair, Anne looks timeless.

©Hever Castle

Book of Hours Room

This room is worth spending a fair amount of time in. Start at the large tapestry which was woven around 1525 and depicts Henry's sister Mary and Louis XII of France's wedding. Anne attended the wedding and is thought to be one of the ladies in the tapestry. We don't know exactly which figure Anne is, but feel free to pick out the one you think she is and for you that will be the reality.

Anne's time in France was very significant. It's where she learned the important things for any woman of the day (manners, fashion, and music.) It was the skills that she learned in France that would set Anne apart from the other women at the English court.

There are two books of hours, or prayer books, in the centre of the room. They are beautiful and expensive books, full of colourful images. Anne probably inherited the books from a relative. The book of hours farthest from the door you came in from is thought to be the very book that Anne took with her to the Tower of London right before she was executed. In it she has written "Remember me when you do pray that hope doth lead from day to day." This is a powerful sentiment from a woman who was preparing emotionally for her death. The prayer book must have been Anne's greatest comfort during her dark days in the Tower. Anne was a deeply spiritual person.

Have a look at the fireplace. Above it you will see Anne and Henry's combined coat of arms. You will also see on either side replica love letters written between them. Not many of Anne's letters to Henry have survived so the print displayed to the right of the fireplace is a real treat. In it Anne speculates that king may have feelings for her due to her placement in Queen Katherine's household:

"The warrant of maid of honour to the Queen induces me to think that your Majesty has some regard for me, since it gives me the means of seeing you oftener, and of assuring you, by my own lips (which I shall do on the first opportunity), that I am your Majesty's very obliged and obedient servant, without any reserve" - Anne Boleyn

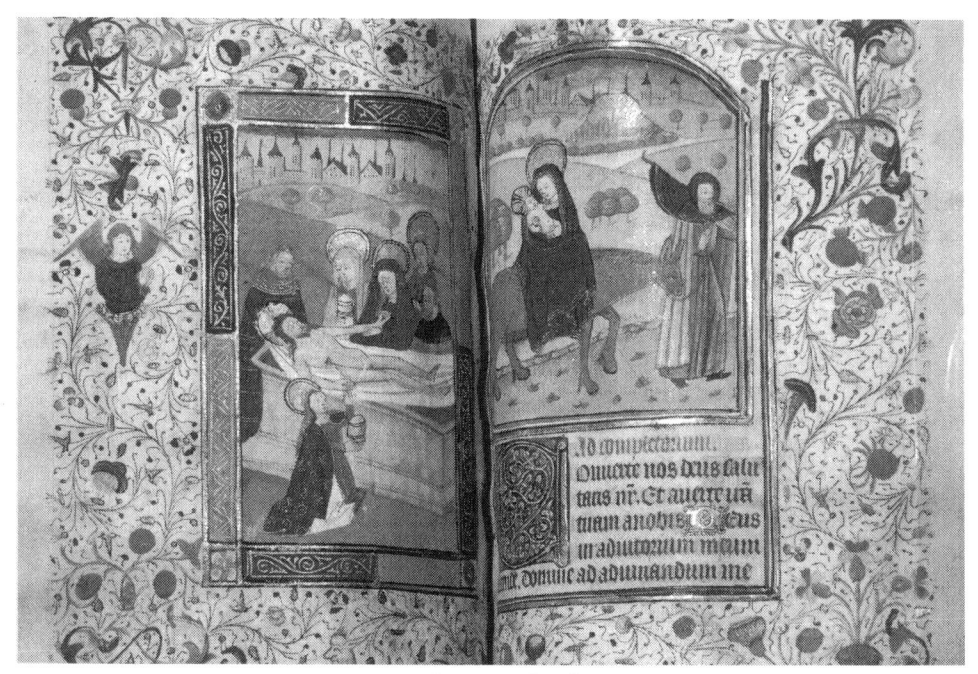

©Hever Castle

Likewise in a reproduction of a letter from Henry to Anne to the left of the fireplace he addresses Anne as his mistress and friend and writes more than a few poetic verses like:

"My heart and I surrender themselves into your hands"

and

"Thus it is with our love: absence has placed distance between us, nevertheless, fervour increases, at least on my part."

Even five hundred years later, the words but can't but make your heart beat a little faster. Take a moment to let the love that Henry and Anne had for each other overwhelm you. Then compose yourself and head to the next room.

©Hever Castle

Queen's Chamber

You may have heard the nursery school rhyme:

"Divorced, beheaded, died. Divorced, beheaded, survived."

If not, it's a good way to remember the outcomes of all six of Henry's marriages. This room is a tribute to Henry's six wives and each has a portrait along the wall. Henry married three Katherines, two Annes, and one Jane (although not in that order). And Katherine Parr was likely named after Katherine of Aragon as her mother was a lady-in-waiting to Henry's first wife. So it's no wonder that Henry married three Katherines. Such a great name, if I do say so myself.

Just like Anne Boleyn there are myths and controversies surrounding the other five of Henry's wives. Let's do a quick roll call:

Katherine of Aragon

Catalina the Infanta of Spain, Princess of Wales

Katherine of Aragon was a fighter. She grew up following her parents Isabella and Ferdinand around while they fought wars against the Moors, united Spain, and restored the Catholic faith. From when she was a mere babe Katherine was betrothed to Arthur, Prince of Wales, heir to the English throne. So Katherine knew very early on that her destiny was to be Queen of England. But it was a rocky road to get there and a rocky road to stay there. Katherine did marry Arthur when they were teenagers, but he died a few months later. She then had to wait a further 7 years to marry Henry VIII while she slipped into poverty. Henry rescued her like a knight in shining armour and they were happily married for over 20 years before Anne Boleyn came along.

Anne Boleyn

Marquis of Pembroke

How do you feel about Anne Boleyn up until now? Do you feel like you're getting to know her?

Jane Seymour

Lady-in-waiting to Katherine of Aragon and Anne Boleyn

Jane was not as well educated as her two predecessors, but she did serve both of them as a lady-in-waiting. Her family was on the rise, and when she became queen, she furthered their cause as well as tried to reconcile Henry with his two children. She had the makings of a good queen. She modelled herself after Katherine of Aragon rather than Anne Boleyn, which isn't surprising. Jane was pious, devout, kind, and a real matriarch. Unfortunately, her life was cut short when she died shortly after giving Henry his much needed male heir, the future King Edward VI. Henry was so distraught that he locked himself up for weeks before he could function as a monarch again. Jane was said to be the love of his life and he chose to be buried next to her at St George's Chapel at Windsor Castle.

Anne of Cleves

Henry may have married his last two wives for passion, but when it came time for his next marriage, he knew that the had to be sensible and make a political alliance. Things were getting tense with France, so Henry looked to the Holy Roman Empire this time, and not Spain or Italy. He went with Germany and the Duchy of Cleves. It was a doomed marriage from the beginning. The pair first met when Henry surprised Anne at Rochester. It was a complete disaster and Henry never really recovered from his first impressions of Anne. He went ahead with the marriage anyways but then couldn't consummate it. He blamed Anne for being ugly and smelly. The only solution was an annulment. Anne got Hever Castle, got to keep her head, and got a new title "King's beloved sister" for the rest of her days. She never remarried (can you blame her?) For more on Anne of Cleves see page 42.

Katherine Howard

Anne Boleyn's cousin, Katherine, was just a teenager when she met the old fat tyrant Henry VIII. In another complete reversal from his last marriage, Henry chose Katherine because he fancied the pants off of her. Although he was unable to consummate his marriage to Anne of Cleves, with little Katherine Howard he had no problem. Like her cousin, Katherine was a lady-in-waiting to her predecessor. She was the third of Henry's wives to play that whole game of wait-on-the-wife-and-steal-the-husband. Also like her cousin, Katherine's marriage to Henry was short-lived. She was accused of adultery and treason (only this time it was more likely to be true) with the dashing courtier Thomas Culpepper. They both lost their heads for it. Finally Katherine followed in her cousin Anne's footsteps by giving the conventional script of execution speeches and departing the world with dignity (she practiced placing her head on the block the night before). Katherine is buried next to Anne Boleyn at St Peter Ad Vincula Chapel.

Katherine Parr

Henry's choice for his sixth wife shows that he'd come full circle. Katherine Parr was very similar to her namesake Katherine of Aragon in education, manners, temperament, although not in religion. She was in her early 30s and about to be widowed for the second time when Henry first met Katherine. Although he quickly fell in love with her, Katherine only had eyes for Thomas Seymour (brother of Henry's third wife Jane). Henry saw what was happening between the two love birds and promptly assigned Thomas to a diplomatic post in Brussels to get him off the scene. Katherine and Henry married in 1543 at Hampton Court Palace. By this time Henry was pretty darn old and perhaps unsurprisingly their marriage did not result in any children. But Katherine was an amiable companion to Henry and they often debated religious theology.

Katherine published two books Psalms or Prayers and Lamentations of a Sinner. This was a tremendous feat for a woman of her time. As queen her court became famous for the excellent education provided to women. When Henry died he provided for her amply but she didn't waste any time marrying her former flame Thomas Seymour. It was a great scandal at court. The couple took in Katherine's step daughter the Lady Elizabeth. Unbeknownst to Katherine, Thomas had proposed to Elizabeth before Katherine but she'd turned him down. So inviting Elizabeth to live with them was a recipe for disaster.

One day Katherine caught her husband and fourteen year old Elizabeth making out in the garden while Katherine was pregnant and so Elizabeth was sent away (for so many reasons). A few months later Katherine died in childbirth but still had time to give her husband an earful on her deathbed. The conversation was not recorded for prosperity. But you can only imagine...

Staircase Gallery

This gallery was built in 1506 by Thomas Boleyn to connect the two wings of the house and give access to the Long Gallery. There are portraits of all of King Henry VIII's children here and they are displayed chronologically in the order in which they were born.

First up is Katherine of Aragon's daughter Queen Mary I (reigned 1553-1558), also known as Bloody Mary because of all of the Protestants who went to the stake during her reign. Her legacy of being the first woman to successfully claim the throne of England, which paved the way for her sister Elizabeth, seems to be overshadowed by the sadness in her life. Mary never forgave her father for destroying her mother and breaking with Rome. She married a Spanish scoundrel, Philip of Spain, and died childless, and alone.

The next two portraits are of Anne's daughter Elizabeth I (reigned 1558-1603). The first is a portrait of Elizabeth as a young girl. When you look at her you can almost imagine all of the teenage angst she must have been going through - having a tenuous relationship with her father, getting a new step mother practically every year, trying to get back into the line of succession. The next portrait of Elizabeth is much more recognisable as it is her as queen.

The last portrait is of Henry's youngest child, King Edward VI (reigned 1547-1553). Poor Edward was just a young boy when he became king. He died as a teenager, an orphan with no love from his remaining family, just uncles using their relationship with him to gain power.

©Hever Castle

The Waldegrave Room

After Anne of Cleves' death, the Waldegrave family acquired Hever Castle. They were Catholic, which wasn't acceptable under King Edward VI. It's ironic that Edward Waldegrave bought the former castle of Anne Boleyn's family considering Anne's role in the demise of Catholicism in England. If Katherine of Aragon had only given Henry a son, then Waldegrave would have been able to practice Catholicism in peace for his whole life.

Edward Waldegrave's fortune rose and fell with the reigns of Henry VIII's children. Under Edward VI, the Waldegraves had to give up practicing Catholicism, or at least put on appearances. When Mary I came to power, Edward was knighted.

Mary briefly brought back Catholicism and Edward got a good deal on Hever Castle. However, in the topsy-turvy world of the Tudor court, when Elizabeth I came to power, Edward lost all of his titles and, like Anne Boleyn, he died in the Tower of London. Edward's son Charles was fortunate to keep Hever Castle, but retired from court life.

To the right of the bed is a tiny chapel called an oratory. It was built in 1584 so that the family could worship in private. Considering its size and the subversive nature of what went on behind the screen, it's an absolutely stunning little room.

In the cabinet by the door there is a very impressive sword called the "Rhyming Blade Sword." It is only one of five of its kind.

Along the wall behind the sword is an introduction to the Stuart family. As Elizabeth I had no children, when she died the English crown passed to her cousin Mary Queen of Scot's child King James IV of Scotland. This united England and Scotland under one ruler and James styled himself "King of Great Britain and Ireland."

The Henry Room

Henry VIII gets his name on this room even if we're not sure if he ever slept in it. Odds are, with this being one of the largest bedrooms in the castle, that he did. The Tudor paneling dates from around 1565 and the ceiling dates from around 1462. The ceiling is the oldest in the castle.

The bed dates from 1540 and is similar to the one that Henry would have preferred. It was very important for the king to like his bed. You wouldn't want a cranky monarch complaining of a backache over breakfast.

During Tudor times, the bed would have been a badge of social status. You had to show that you could afford the best bed. Sir Thomas Boleyn would have also made sure that the wall hangings contained Henry's royal colours of green and white with the Tudor rose embroidered on them.

Long Gallery

This is the longest room in the castle. Take a good look. From the doorway in which you enter the view down the room shows how small Hever Castle really is!

Thomas Boleyn built the room in 1506 as a meeting place for his friends and family. It was also meant as an exercise room so think of it like a Tudor gym. Although they wouldn't have had stair masters or elliptical machines back then, walking up and down this room in the winter time would have been far more pleasant than strolling through the mud and rain outside in the gardens.

Henry VIII sometimes held court in this room in the alcove. The portraits on the wall when you enter the room are a tribute to his ancestors. First up is his paternal grandmother Margaret Beaufort. She was as formidable as she was pious. Next there's a portrait of the king's mother, Elizabeth of York. In contrast to her mother-in-law, Elizabeth was sweet natured and easy-going. Poor Henry was only 11 when his mother passed away. He would spend the rest of his life measuring up his wives to the high standard set by his mother.

Along the plaster on the walls of this room you'll see Henry and Anne's initials "HR" (Latin for King Henry was Henricius Rex) and "AB" (obviously for Anne Boleyn). If you're struggling to make out the "HR," it's because the top loop and vertical stem of the "R" are shared with the "H." You'd also be forgiven if you thought the initials were "ER" for Anne's daughter Elizabeth I (Elizabeth Regina.)

Make your way down the long room and stop at the window closest to the door. Look up at the window and you'll see the name, year, and coat of arms of Hever Castle's owners. The first recorded owner was William de Hever circa 1200. If you follow the windows along the wall back in the direction you came from you can see the full history of Hever Castle's owners. When you get back to the door in which you entered from you'll see the last window Edmund Meade Waldo 1896. Ironically William Waldorf Astor didn't put his own name up there. Maybe he ran out of space.

In order to continue your tour, cross the length of the room for the last time. Stop and admire anything that you want to see more closely that you didn't during your initial pass of the room. For example, a replica of the last letter that Anne wrote to Henry on the wall in between the last two alcoves is heartwarming.

After you leave the room, walk along the corridor and pass by the teeny tiny bedrooms where Lord Astor's daughters slept during the flood of 1968. They don't look very comfortable but when you have water in your home more than waist high, desperate times call for desperate measures.

Astor Suite

Here we have front and centre a portrait of the man who made it his mission to restore Hever Castle to the beauty and splendour you see today - William Waldorf Astor. Not only did he make the castle pretty and habitable, he also added modern conveniences that we take for granted today like electricity, heating, and a sewage system. The bathrooms also had modern plumbing installed. Astor didn't do a bad job balancing the tricky business of making the castle modern but keeping with the authenticity of the Tudor era. Look very carefully to see if you can spot an electricity socket on the wall.

Winston Churchill was a neighbour of the Astors. He lived five miles down the road at Chartwell (now a National Heritage site which also merits a visit). Since Churchill was such a good mate of the Astors, he sent William's son John Jacob a painting set which you can see here. John Jacob was an avid painter.

There was one Astor who didn't get along with Churchill and that was Nancy Astor, William's daughter-in-law. Nancy was a member of Parliament (MP) and a woman (obviously) who butted heads with Churchill over the fact that he didn't think women belonged in government. Nancy was rumoured once to have said to Churchill "If you were my husband, I would poison your tea" to which Churchill retorted "if you were my wife Nancy, I'd drink it!"

Pick up the telephone on the table and listen to the current Lord Astor explain what it was like growing up at Hever Castle, especially during the flood of 1968.

Pass through the door into the smaller room. Take a look at the guest lists of all of the famous people that partied with the Astors in Hever Castle. Do you recognise any of the names?

Council Chamber

And here we end our tour in the oldest part of the castle - the Council Chamber which dates back to around 1270. The castle's first inhabitants would have used this room for practically everything - eating, sleeping, entertaining, and even going to the bathroom. Hopefully not all at the same time! Check out the primitive toilet behind the door you entered through. It would have been a bit chilly in winter as it opened onto the moat where the waste would have fallen.

Other primitive remnants of the original castle include the chains which operated the portcullis. If any invaders rode up to the castle on horseback, the gate could be quickly dropped so that they couldn't get in. The rest of the stuff in this room is rather gruesome. If you have the stomach for it, check out the old knives used for beheading. Don't worry, Anne got a much nicer one than these. She had a top executioner with a top sword come all of the way from Calais to do her the honours.

Tudor Village

Alas we have reached the end of our tour of Hever Castle! I know it's sad. If you're lucky enough to be an overnight guest staying at the luxury bed and breakfast, then you can go on to explore the Tudor Village. It was built by William Waldorf Astor and it is connected to the main part of the castle through an underground tunnel. If you are not an overnight guest, there's still plenty more of Hever to explore outside.

The castle has fantastic grounds including an Italian garden and maze. Stroll by the man-made lake, another addition to the castle made by William Waldorf Astor. If you'd like to read more on Hever Castle owners Anne of Cleves and William Waldorf Astor, keep reading. Don't miss the resources on the last page and sign up for the Eventful Travel e-mail newsletter to receive more information on other books in the Castles and Countesses series.

Anne of Cleves

Henry VIII gave his fourth wife, Anne of Cleves, Hever Castle in 1540. She lived there happily for almost 20 years up, until her death in 1557. Anne of Cleves had every reason to be happy. She survived her marriage to Henry while keeping her head on her shoulders and she got to live in a beautiful castle. Her fate was a strong contrast to that of Anne Boleyn.

Anne of Cleves and Anne Boleyn had a lot in common, besides their first name. They were both reformers, they were both quite attractive, even if not in the same standards of the time (Henry fell in love with Anne of Cleves after seeing her portrait and Anne Boleyn had a spunky personality and alluring brown eyes), and they both had failed marriages to the same cantankerous tyrant. But there the similarities ended. Anne Boleyn had a fiery personality and strong opinions, which she voiced to everyone. In contrast, Anne of Cleves was submissive and pragmatic.

The Annes' marriages to Henry couldn't have been more different either. Henry fell in love with Anne Boleyn deeply and over many years. They were a true love match and Henry practically destroyed his own country in order to marry her. Anne of Cleves was selected to be Henry's fourth wife because the union suited a diplomatic need for an Anglo-German alliance.

Anna von Jülich-Kleve-Berg was born in 1515 near Düsseldorf. Her parents were John III, Duke of Jülich, Cleves and Berg, an important German ruler, and Maria of Jülich-Berg. For ease, we'll keep referring to her as Anne of Cleves. Anne descended from Edward I on her mother's side, and was closely related to Louis XII of France and the Duke of Burgundy on her father's. Anne was very sheltered during her upbringing. Her older sister, Sybille, was married off to John Frederick I, Elector of Saxony and Head of the Protestant Confederation of Germany in 1526. Likewise, Anne was betrothed to Francis, the heir of the Duke of Lorraine, the following year.

The marriage to Francis was arranged by Anne's father, however when he passed away, Anne's brother cancelled the arrangement. The new duke refused to give up the territory of Guelders to the Duke of Lorraine in 1539. Proverbial battle lines were drawn and Anne had to forget about Francis.

Two years after the death of his beloved third wife Jane Seymour, Henry VIII was looking for a new foreign bride to help build diplomatic relations. Cleves was always on Henry's radar, even 10 years prior when he was determined to marry Anne Boleyn. Although Henry had never laid eyes on Anne of Cleves, she ticked all of the boxes on paper. To seal the deal, Henry sent his painter Hans Holbein to paint a portrait of Anne of Cleves so that he could see what Anne looked like before he agreed to marry her. Allegedly he fell in love with Anne's portrait. The proposed union seemed promising.

By the end of September 1539, a marriage treaty between England and Cleves had been agreed and preparations were made for Anne to travel to England. But it all went downhill from there. Being impatient to meet his lovely bride, and in the great tradition of courtly love, Henry set out to meet Anne on her way to London. She never saw him coming.

Henry's plan was to intercept Anne in disguise. Anne would instantly see through the disguise and fall passionately into his arms. There would probably be kissing and hugging too. But it went more like this:

- Henry ambushed Anne at Rochester

- Anne did not recognise Henry and was appalled at a total stranger being so familiar with her

- Henry's ego was wounded

- Henry declared "I like her not" but went ahead with the marriage anyways

- When Henry couldn't consummate the marriage he blamed his advisors, including his chief advisor Oliver Cromwell, for misleading him about Anne's appearance

- Anne was offered an annulment

- With no other option Anne accepted the arrangement

- Anne kept her head, although Cromwell did not

Start to finish, the series of events took place over six months. Anne's demotion from queen to "King's Beloved Sister" was a blessing in disguise. Anne didn't have to deal with Henry's dangerously moody personality or stinky rotting leg and she was held in standing only second to Henry's later wives and daughters, not to mention property like Hever Castle and Richmond Palace. Later when Henry's fifth wife, Katherine Howard, was beheaded, Anne's brother the Duke of Cleves pushed Henry to take Anne back. He refused.

Some say that Anne was a little jealous of Henry's last wife, Katherine Parr, who was five years older and not famous for her beauty. But Anne did outlive Katherine, and all of the rest of Henry's wives. Although for the record, Katherine of Aragon lived the longest of Henry's wives as she was near fifty at the time of her death, whereas Anne of Cleves was 41.

Anne of Cleves

William Waldorf Astor & Restoration

Throughout the twentieth century, the Astor family and Hever Castle played an important part in politics. They also threw lots of parties. But what possessed a New Yorker to buy up and renovate an English Castle?

William Waldorf Astor was born in New York City in 1848, but spent his childhood in Germany and Italy. He returned to New York to study at Columbia Law School and started his career in law. He also worked in his father John Jacob Astor III's real estate business.

William Waldorf Astor

A little while later Astor thought he found his true vocation as a politician and entered the New York State Assembly as a Republican. However, his father died in 1890 which made him the richest man in America at that time. He built the Waldorf

Astoria hotel with his cousin John Jacob Astor IV.

A family feud in 1891 was the last straw for Astor in New York so he packed up wife Mary, and their children, and moved to England. In 1892 Astor faked his own death by leaking to the American media that he had died of pneumonia. The ruse didn't last long but it was pretty funny. All of the press were laughing when they found out. Astor was the only one who didn't think it was funny.

In 1899 Astor became a British citizen. He bought up a few properties in the UK and opened the Waldorf Hotel in London in 1906. However, the real shining jewel in his property collection was Hever Castle, which he bought in 1903.

Astor was a huge philanthropist. He gave to countless charities, hospitals, and colleges. In recognition, King George V gave Astor the title of Baron Astor of Hever Castle. The following year he was promoted from Baron to Viscount. The haters claimed that Astor bought himself his title (which he kind of did indirectly but who wouldn't if they could?)

Astor's daughter-in-law Nancy was a force to be reckoned with. She became the first woman to sit in the UK Parliament. Considering her gender and the fact that she was from Virginia, you can image how this went down in an institution older than 700 years old at the time. Nancy was a double whammy - a woman and an American.

Note - the first woman actually elected to Parliament was Constance Markievicz from the constituency Dublin St Patrick's. However she was too busy doing jail time for her militant actions and in line with Sinn Féin (Irish Republican political party) policies, Constances declined to take her seat in Parliament.

Nancy, by contrast, was you might say softer as a woman compared to Constance. Although her tongue was as sharp as Constance's shooting skills. Nancy was alleged to have said a lot of outlandish things in her day but here's just one little gem. On hearing of the death of one of her political opponents Nancy looked pleased. When she was called out on her insensitivity, Nancy allegedly replied "I'm a Virginian. We shoot to kill."

Nancy Astor circa 1908 Library of Congress

Nancy served in Parliament from the end of World War I to the end of World War II. She became unpopular during World War II because of her opposition to it, which indirectly implied that she was sympathetic to Hitler. By 1945 both her husband and her party were against her. She left politics kicking and screaming.

Nancy was quite a colourful lady and you can see now the types of people that the Astors would have mingled with. They were the toast of the town and hobnobbed with the politicians and celebrities of their day - Bernard Shaw, Douglas Fairbanks, and Harold McMillan to name a few. The weekend parties that the Astors threw at Hever Castle during the twentieth century were legendary.

Unfortunately, all good things must come to an end. The Astor family sold Hever

Castle to a privately held company called Broadland Properties Ltd in 1983. Although Hever Castle would no longer be a family home, it would finally be open to the public to visit. And thank goodness for that!

Resources

Come and share with us your thoughts, feelings, and opinions on social media:

www.facebook.com/eventfultravel

@eventfultravel

www.eventful-travel.com

Make sure to sign up for the Eventful Travel e-mail list at www.eventful-travel.com so that you can get the scoop on more Castles and Countesses guides and free stuff!

For an extensive encyclopaedia on all things Anne Boleyn, check out www.theanneboleynfiles.com, which is a collection of blog posts on all things Anne Boleyn and spans many years. The website is a labour of love for author and Anne Boleyn advocate Claire Ridgeway.

During your visit to Hever Castle, you can rent an audio guide that will take you on a tour of the castle. The same content is available in the UK iTunes store as an iPhone application. The iPhone app is actually cheaper than the audio guide and you can listen to the content over and over again. If you have a US iTunes account, sorry it's not available to you (unless you have a super technical member of your family who can figure out how to switch your accounts just to purchase the app and then switch back). Sadly, I can't figure it out myself.

www.hevercastle.co.uk - official website of Hever Castle

www.eventful-travel.com - official website of the Castles and Countesses tour guides

Books

Weir, Alison (2007). The Six Wives of Henry VIII. London: Vintage. ISBN 9780099523628.

Weir, Alison (2010). The Lady in the Tower: The Fall of Anne Boleyn. London: Vintage. ISBN 9780712640176.

Ives, Eric (2005). The Life and Death of Anne Boleyn: The Most Happy. Oxford: Blackwell Publishing. ISBN 9781405134637.

Starkey, David (2004). Six Wives: The Queens of Henry VIII. London: Vintage. ISBN 9780099437246